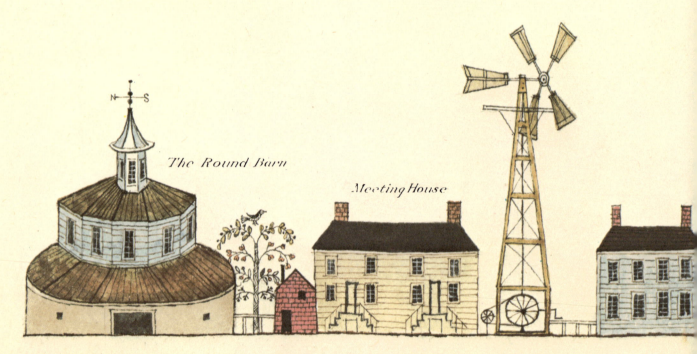

The Round Barn

Meeting House

Puffin Books

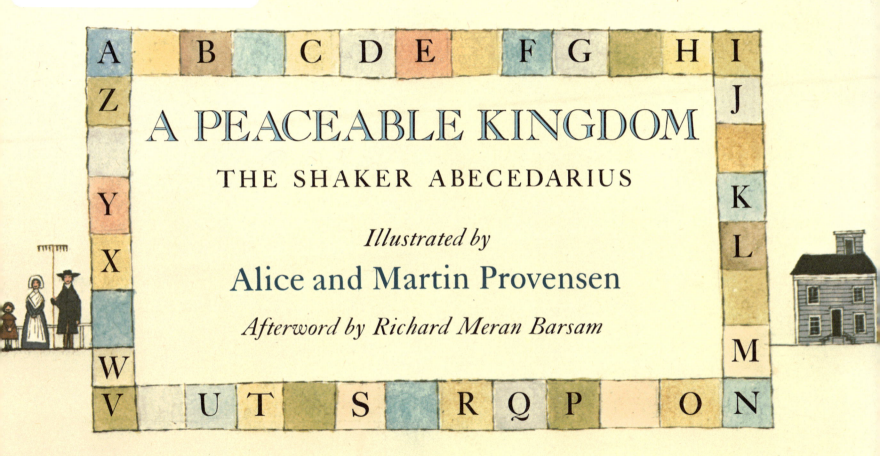

A PEACEABLE KINGDOM

THE SHAKER ABECEDARIUS

Illustrated by

Alice and Martin Provensen

Afterword by Richard Meran Barsam

Penguin Books Ltd, Harmondsworth, Middlesex, England
Penguin Books, 625 Madison Avenue, New York, New York 10022, U.S.A.
Penguin Books Australia Ltd, Ringwood, Victoria, Australia
Penguin Books Canada Limited, 2801 John Street, Markham, Ontario, Canada L3R 1B4
Penguin Books (N.Z.) Ltd, 182–190 Wairau Road, Auckland 10, New Zealand

First published in the United States of America by The Viking Press, 1978
First published in Great Britain by Kestrel Books, 1978
Published in Picture Puffins, 1981
Reprinted 1982
Illustrations copyright © Alice and Martin Provensen, 1978
Afterword copyright © Richard Meran Barsam, 1978
All rights reserved
Library of Congress Cataloging in Publication Data
Main entry under title: A Peaceable kingdom.
Published in Shaker Manifesto of July 1882 under title: Rhymes of animals.
Summary: An illustrated alphabet rhyme that includes the animals from alligator to zebra.
1. Alphabet rhymes. 2. Children's poetry,
American. [1. Alphabet. 2. Animals—Poetry]
I. Provensen, Alice. II. Provensen, Martin.
[PS991.A1R47 1981] [811] 80-24866 ISBN 0-14-050370-6 (pbk.)

Printed in the United States of America
by Rae Publishing Co., Inc., Cedar Grove, New Jersey

THE SHAKER ABECEDARIUS

ALLIGATOR, Beetle, Porcupine, Whale,
BOBOLINK, Panther, Dragonfly, Snail,
CROCODILE, Monkey, Buffalo, Hare,
DROMEDARY, Leopard, Mud Turtle, Bear,
ELEPHANT, Badger, Pelican, Ox,
FLYING FISH, Reindeer, Anaconda, Fox,
GUINEA PIG, Dolphin, Antelope, Goose,
HUMMINGBIRD, Weasel, Pickerel, Moose,
IBEX, Rhinoceros, Owl, Kangaroo,
JACKAL, Opposum, Toad, Cockatoo,
KINGFISHER, Peacock, Anteater, Bat,
LIZARD, Ichneumon, Honeybee, Rat,
MOCKINGBIRD, Camel, Grasshopper, Mouse,

NIGHTINGALE, Spider, Cuttlefish, Grouse,
OCELOT, Pheasant, Wolverine, Auk,
PERIWINKLE, Ermine, Katydid, Hawk,
QUAIL, Hippopotamus, Armadillo, Moth,
RATTLESNAKE, Lion, Woodpecker, Sloth,
SALAMANDER, Goldfinch, Angleworm, Dog,
TIGER, Flamingo, Scorpion, Frog,
UNICORN, Ostrich, Nautilus, Mole,
VIPER, Gorilla, Basilisk, Sole,
WHIPPOORWILL, Beaver, Centipede, Fawn,
XANTHOS, Canary, Polliwog, Swan,
YELLOWHAMMER, Eagle, Hyena, Lark,
ZEBRA, Chameleon, Butterfly, Shark.

—from The Shaker Manifesto, 1882

A

LLIGATOR, Beetle

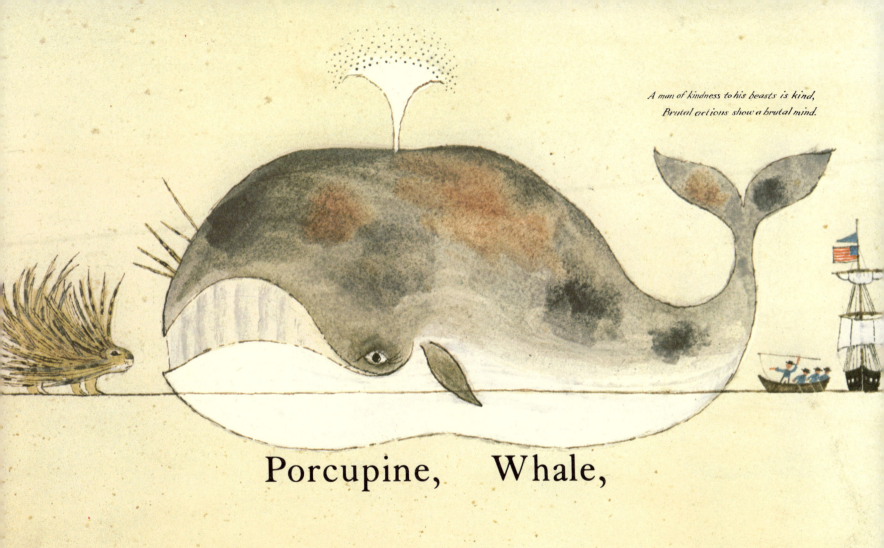

A man of kindness to his beasts is kind,
Brutal actions show a brutal mind.

Porcupine,   Whale,

I am the trumpet of Wisdom.

BOBOLINK,   Panther,

Thee sees we love our garden...

Dragonfly, Snail,

C

ROCODILE,

Monkey, Buffalo, Hare,

D

ROMEDARY,

Leopard,　　Mud Turtle,　　Bear,

I am Strength. I am Power. I am comfort every hour.

ELEPHANT, Badger,

Pelican,   Ox,

Wings of Holy Wisdom.

FLYING FISH,   Reindeer,

I comfort the weak and strengthen the wise.

Anaconda,   Fox,

GUINEA PIG,

Dolphin,   Antelope,   Goose,

Hummingbird,

Weasel, Pickerel, Moose,

IBEX,   Rhinoceros,

Owl,   Kangaroo,

This is an emblem of My Love. Receive it from My Little Dove.

JACKAL, Oppossum,

Sweet Peace and Heavenly Love, I bear on my wings from Heaven above.

SHAKER HERB TEA

ROOTS AND HERBS SHAKER

Toad,   Cockatoo,

KINGFISHER,

Peacock,   Anteater,   Bat,

L

IZARD,

Ichneumon, Honeybee, Rat,

Come play upon my harp of Joy...

M OCKINGBIRD,

Camel, Grasshopper, Mouse

...and dance before the Lord.

NIGHTINGALE,

Spider,   Cuttlefish,   Grouse,

O CELOT,

Pheasant, Wolverine, Auk,

P

ERIWINKLE,

Ermine,   Katydid,   Hawk,

QUAIL,   Hippopotamus,

Blow ye My trumpet in Zion and awake all sleeping souls.

Armadillo,   Moth,

Beneath this branch of Purity,
Do come and sit, and sup with me.

Rattlesnake,   Lion,

Labor is truly made Worship.

Woodpecker,   Sloth,

Come gather under my wings of peace.

S

ALAMANDER,

Goldfinch,   Angleworm,   Dog,

TIGER,

Flamingo, Scorpion, Frog,

NICORN,

Ostrich,   Nautilus,   Mole,

Mother Lucy's table of fruit.

VIPER,

Gorilla,   Basilisk,   Sole,

W

HIPPOORWILL,

Beaver,   Centipede,   Fawn,

Whoever makes a thing more bright, He is an angel of all light.

Xanthos,

Canary, Polliwog, Swan,

Y ELLOWHAMMER, Eagle,

I am a Dove of Comfort and Love

Hyena,   Lark,

Z EBRA,

Chameleon,   Butterfly,   Shark.

AFTERWORD

Shaker children must have had a rollicking good time as they recited their way through this alphabet verse, or abecedarius, an incongruous world of animals created for the practical purpose of teaching reading. The rhyme and meter helped students to learn and turned a chore into a pleasurable activity.

Shaker education was simple, limited mostly to those practical skills that would help the children to become active members in the life of the community. Their schoolteachers were strict in matters of discipline, but the Shakers loved song, dance, and mime, and these pleasures were part of school life.

The Shakers behaved soberly, but they were not dull, and the stern codes that regulated their communal life in matters of worship, dress, and eating did not restrict the human spirit. That may help to explain why this animal alphabet is so whimsical and so appealing today, almost one hundred years after its appearance in the Shaker Manifesto of 1882. At home and in school Shaker children learned about barnyard animals, but with this delightful alphabet, they could also roam with the mythical Xanthos, the ichneumon, and the basilisk. Their education may have been simple, but evidently it was fun as well.

The ideals of plainness, harmony, and utility governed all Shaker activities. Their belief in economic, racial, religious, and sexual equality attracted thousands of people to their communities from their founding in 1774 to their high point in 1850. Despite their early prosperity, the Shakers steadily declined. They tried to be self-sufficient, but unwise speculation in land and other bad investments forced them to trade with the outside world.

In 1821 the death of their leader, Mother Lucy, left them without a spiritual guide, dividing and exposing their communities to public scrutiny and some violent reaction. Growth from within was impossible because the Shakers banned marriage and sexual relations, and new members joined sporadically as fewer and fewer outsiders heard the direct call from God that the Shakers believed was conditional to membership. From 6000 members in 1850, the sect declined to only 1700 members in 1900. In 1957 the Shakers stopped admitting new members, thereby ending their organized search for the perfect society. The last male Shaker died in 1960, and by 1976 there were only several elderly female members left.

Today people remain interested in the Shakers, and a flourishing museum in Hancock, Massachusetts, preserves the furniture, buildings, and life-style of one of their communities. A visit there provides a rich insight into a simple culture. When outsiders criticized the limited education of Shaker children, they must have overlooked this alphabet, for it continues to delight the imagination and curiosity of all children.

Richard Meran Barsam